To Phoebe, my little Leo pug who faithfully kept
my lap warm while I wrote this thing.

Aadamsmedia
Adams Media
An Imprint of Simon & Schuster, Inc.
100 Technology Center Drive
Stoughton, Massachusetts 02072

Copyright © 2022 by Simon & Schuster, Inc.

First Adams Media hardcover edition
October 2022

ADAMS MEDIA and colophon are
trademarks of Simon & Schuster.

For information about special discounts for
bulk purchases, please contact Simon &
Schuster Special Sales at 1-866-506-1949
or business@simonandschuster.com.

The Simon & Schuster Speakers Bureau can
bring authors to your live event. For more
information or to book an event contact the
Simon & Schuster Speakers Bureau at
1-866-248-3049 or visit our website at
www.simonspeakers.com.

Interior design by Priscilla Yuen
Interior illustrations by Evgeniya Oparina
and Jamie Kazmercyk
Interior images © 123RF/troyka;
Simon & Schuster, Inc.

Manufactured in China

10 9 8 7 6 5 4 3 2 1

Library of Congress Cataloging-in-
Publication Data
Names: Robinson, Syd, author.
Title: Who do the stars say you are? /
Syd Robinson.
Description: First Adams Media hardcover
edition. | Stoughton, Massachusetts:
Adams Media, 2022
Identifiers: LCCN 2022006123 |
ISBN 9781507218419 (hc) |
ISBN 9781507218426 (ebook)
Subjects: LCSH: Astrology. |
Stars--Miscellanea.
Classification: LCC BF1728.A2 R59 2022 |
DDC 133.5--dc23/eng/20220304
LC record available at
https://lccn.loc.gov/2022006123

ISBN 978-1-5072-1841-9
ISBN 978-1-5072-1842-6 (ebook)

CONTENTS

Introduction • 5

CHAPTER 1
Get to Know the Signs • 7

CHAPTER 2
The Signs and Their Relationships • 33

CHAPTER 3
The Signs and Their Families • 53

CHAPTER 4
The Signs and Their Friends • 71

CHAPTER 5
The Signs and Their Pets • 89

CHAPTER 6
The Signs and Their Homes • 109

CHAPTER 7
The Signs and Their Jobs • 131

CHAPTER 8
The Signs and Food • 151

CHAPTER 9
The Signs and Random Things • 171
(Because...Why Not?)

✳

INTRODUCTION

Maybe you already know that astrology can tell you what signs you're most compatible with or what jobs would be best for you. But did you know that you can learn so much more? Aren't you kinda curious about what type of dog or which iconic movie character you'd be—according to your sign, of course? Maybe you're more interested in what comfort food matches your zodiac traits or who your sign would be in a group chat. (Are you the one always asking for relationship advice? The more sporadic responder?)

In *Who Do the Stars Say You Are?*, you'll find out the answers to these questions and more, with one hundred charts (and tons of super cute illustrations!) to guide the way. Organized into topics like romantic relationships, family, friends, jobs, and home life (and all the random stuff in between, of course!!!), the charts in each chapter will reveal key insights into how each sign would act or identify in a specific, and all-too-relatable, situation. You'll learn:

- How Aries would act when meeting their significant other's parents for the first time
- Which weird relative every Virgo seems to have blocked on social media
- The oddly niche job you'd be surprisingly good at, given that you're a Cancer
- Which non-conventional pet is *so* Capricorn
- The one sign Sagittarius always seems to attract for some reason

Flip through the charts by yourself or with friends, or, hey, leave it out on your coffee table as the perfect conversation starter! However you use this book is entirely up to you, but you're sure to find yourself nodding along—or even agreeing out loud with a "Hey, that sounds just like me!"

And if you want to learn a bit more about a specific zodiac sign, check out the first chapter. There you'll find out what it actually means to be a lionhearted Leo, a comfort-crazed Taurus, or a sensual Scorpio. You'll also discover zodiac bingo cards to help you get to know your sign (and the sign of anyone in your life) even better—and make a fun game out of it. Challenge your friends, family, or maybe even your crush to see who is the *most* like their sign.

From identifying each sign on a first date to figuring out the perfect midnight snacks for your Gemini bestie, it's time to *really* get to know each sign. So let's get down to the juicy stuff: Who do the stars say *you* are?

✴

CHAPTER 1

Get to Know the Signs

So, let me guess: You're sick of people saying, "You're such a [insert sign here]!" and having no idea what they mean by it? Was it a compliment? A jab? A little bit of both? Well, lucky for you, this chapter will give you a bit more insight. And not just into your own sign, but into the signs of everyone in your life! Have you ever wondered why your Virgo boss is like *that*? Or why your Taurus friend always wants to stay in on a Friday night? Or maybe why that Scorpio you matched with on Bumble is so *irresistibly snackalicious*?!

This chapter contains descriptions of each of the twelve sun signs, as well as cute bingo boards that you can play by yourself or with others. See how many of the boxes you tick in your own sign, or have your friend/relative/crush/whoever look at their sign's bingo board and compare results. No matter how you play, you're sure to find out something about yourself or each other in this chapter...just sayin'!

ARIES

MARCH 21–APRIL 19

As the first sign of the zodiac, Aries are natural-born leaders. Aries is a fire sign, meaning that the people born under this sign have an undeniable passionate, burning energy to them. They're creative, excitable, childlike, and ambitious. They're almost always down for different adventures, but can be a little domineering when it comes to executing these plans—and most other things. Represented by the ram, they like to do things their own way and are willing to butt heads with anything blocking their path. These rams are also known for being a bit hot-headed, but that's only because they're so self-assured!

STRENGTHS	WEAKNESSES	MOST COMPATIBLE WITH
Creative	Impatient	Leo
Ambitious	Stubborn	Sagittarius
Honest	Impulsive	Gemini
Determined	Irritable	Libra
Independent	Selfish	Aquarius

ARIES BINGO

Impulse buys a shirt	Gets overly competitive at otherwise chill board game nights	*Rage cries*	Still has childhood trophies on prominent display	"I'm bored. Let's go."
Has a different crush every fifteen minutes	Downloads a meditation app	Deletes meditation app for more storage	Gets bored of the shirt they impulse bought	"I don't get why everyone thinks I'm intimidating..."
Secretly loves that everyone thinks they're intimidating	Tracks package immediately after placing an order	FREE SPACE to get really mad about something	Gases up their friends constantly	"I just wanna make out with a stranger!!!!!!!"
Refreshes package tracking page again	Befriends any and every person in the bar bathroom	*Will* flirt with their friends' hot older siblings, and that's a promise	Always has random bruises	Forgets what they were mad about
Only plays hype rap music when they're handed the AUX	"Can I pet your dog?!?!?!?!"	No deeper loathing than for slow walkers	Palpable god complex	Impulse buys another shirt

♉ TAURUS

APRIL 20–MAY 20

As an earth sign, Taureans are known for their perseverance, stability, and stubbornness—*ooooh*, are they stubborn—much like their symbol, the bull! (But, to be fair, most Taureans would probably argue that they just know what they want and aren't afraid to make it known.) They love the finer things in life, like good food, art, and culture. This makes being, or even just knowing, a Taurus a five-star experience in and of itself! On the other hand, Taureans can also get stuck in patterns that feel safe and familiar. Same thing goes for when they're in love: Taureans will stand by you and won't waver, even when things get tough. Basically, if you're looking for the most dependable zodiac folks, look no further than Taurus.

STRENGTHS	WEAKNESSES	MOST COMPATIBLE WITH
Reliable	Stubborn	Capricorn
Logical	Materialistic	Virgo
Moral	Addictive	Cancer
Luxurious	Lazy	Scorpio
Patient	Antiprogressive	Pisces

TAURUS BINGO

Has three-hundred-thread-count sheets	"I'm a plant parent."	Wishes Snuggies were still a thing	Always knows the best restaurants	Dedicated to The Cozy Aesthetic™
Loiters in the Target candle aisle	*Fuzzy. Socks.*	Collects stamps or something else oddly specific	Territorial over part of the couch	Buys more plants
Takes a midday nap	Rewatches a comfort show	FREE SPACE to cancel plans	Stays in and watches *Love Island* ♥	Romanticizes autumn
Out-cooks the Barefoot Contessa herself	Takes bubble baths feat. bath bombs, obvi	Loathes—like, *loathes*—itchy clothing tags	Strong distaste for overhead lighting	Has an elaborate skincare routine
Really into bullet journaling lately	Oversized sweaters ⌄⌄ all other clothes	Has big Ferdinand the Bull energy	Makes really cool art low-key	"Quality over quantity!"

♊

GEMINI

MAY 21–JUNE 20

Geminis—the first of the air signs—can be found on the VIP list of just about every social event ever. The socialites of the zodiac, Geminis are friendly, animated, and clever. Symbolized by the twins, Geminis sometimes get a bad rap for appearing "two-faced." But as any Gemini would tell you, they're just good at adapting in different social situations! Geminis thrive when they're able to show off their sparkling wit, and when they get to hang out with people who can verbally spar with them on their level.

STRENGTHS	WEAKNESSES	MOST COMPATIBLE WITH
Hilarious	Fickle	Libra
Witty	Gossipy	Aquarius
In-the-know	Unreliable	Aries
Charismatic	Nosy	Leo
Versatile	Restless	Sagittarius

GEMINI BINGO

First user-name ever was like "xxh0tti3lu-vr44xx"	Checks gossip columns religiously	Flirts through wit and wit only	Always has a ton of *Instagram* stories	*Blocked*
"OMG, did you hear???"	Has fifteen crushes at once	Ringleader of the Group Chat™	"I'm bored."	Views making out like shaking hands
Downloads dating apps	Was definitely on the prom committee	FREE SPACE to post another *Instagram* story	Borderline unhealthy obsession with reality TV	Delivers absolute zingers when need be
Changes the subject in a conversation	Deletes dating apps	Has a questionable search history	Is in at least two *Twitter* feuds	Currently has fifty+ Internet tabs open
Likely to be an RA in college	"I wasn't flirting; I'm just nice!"	Redownloads dating apps	The party host with the most!!!!!!!	The Original Influencer™

CANCER

JUNE 21–JULY 22

Best known for their natural ability to care for others, Cancers are some of the most empathetic people you'll ever meet. Represented by the crab, these emotional water signs go above and beyond for the ones they love, and hold family in especially high regard. Most Cancers will feel a natural calling to be a parent—or if not to be a parent, to fill some role where they can directly support those in need. However, being super emotional can also have its dark side. Lots of Cancers can be overly sensitive, moody, and sometimes even spiteful. But at their best, once you get past the crabs' exterior shells, Cancers' hearts are some of the biggest, mushiest-gushiest things in the world, and they deserve to be regarded as the iconic love machines that they are. Basically, we do not deserve this sign!

STRENGTHS	WEAKNESSES	MOST COMPATIBLE WITH
Nurturing	Moody	Scorpio
Empathetic	Pessimistic	Pisces
Devoted	Passive-aggressive	Taurus
Intuitive	Clingy	Virgo
Giving	Overly sensitive	Capricorn

CANCER BINGO

Angry cries	The Mom/Dad/Parent Friend™	Low-key a hoarder	Obsessed with tiny baby shoes	Uncompromising when need be
Was/is probably a camp counselor	Weirdly good at braiding hair...?	Attends Zoom therapy sessions	Googles Crock-Pot recipes	Can't watch rom-coms without sobbing
Saves every birthday card ever	"Wanna see my future wedding *Pinterest* board?!"	FREE SPACE to cry as a release	*Anxiety!!!!!!!*	Drafts long texts in the Notes app
Randomly bakes cookies at 2 a.m.	Can quote *The Notebook* word for word	"Should I text my ex?"	Texts their ex	Scream-sings Taylor Swift songs
Drives a Subaru	Has an obsession with floral-scented candles	Definitely played mermaids as a kid	Has a niche hobby, like crocheting	*Handmade gifts for everyone!!!*

♌

LEO

JULY 23–AUGUST 22

Diva. Showstopping. Life of the party. All of these things are basically synonymous with Leo, a.k.a. the lion of the zodiac. Ruled by the fire element (and the Sun!), it should come as no surprise that Leos shine with enough heat and ferocity to sustain all life on earth. These celestial lions crave the spotlight more than any other sign, and frankly, they belong in it. Most Leos feel an innate calling to some type of performing arts, public speaking, or anything else that involves a stage of some sort. Sure, these interests can come with a bit of an ego or even vanity, but at their core, Leos are big-hearted, passionate people who love deeply and live to entertain!

STRENGTHS	WEAKNESSES	MOST COMPATIBLE WITH
Charming	Self-involved	Aries
Outgoing	Overly dramatic	Sagittarius
Driven	Arrogant	Gemini
Inviting	Possessive	Libra
Confident	Bossy	Aquarius

LEO BINGO

Former-child-actor energy	Probably has a lion tattoo somewhere	*Loud*	Gradually gets even *louder*	"My birthday is the best holiday!"
A natural-born performer	(Or, at least thinks they are a natural-born performer)	Attention ⌄⌄ their next breath	Rejects monotony in every facet	"Let's make a TikTok!"
Feels spiritually aligned with Pomeranians	Speeds through a stoplight	FREE SPACE to humblebrag	Camera roll is 99.9 percent selfies	"I've always felt famous."
Has glitter in weird places	Gets free stuff for being hot	Posts another selfie to *Instagram*	Will go *out* out anytime, anywhere	Is show-stopping. Original. *Theee* moment.
Checks *Instagram* likes on their new selfie	Favorite vacation is a power trip	Fiercely loyal—like, *fiercely*	The Hot Friend™	Stares at self in mirror

♍ VIRGO

AUGUST 23–SEPTEMBER 22

Detail-oriented, *logical*, and *determined* are typically the first words that come to mind when thinking about Virgos. These earth signs are masterminds when it comes to planning, and they love seeing all their hard work come to fabulous fruition! Symbolized by the virgin, they are endearingly tenderhearted and usually put others first, and are typically pretty sweet and shy. They're predisposed to workaholism, and as they're analytical and sometimes even a bit judgmental, they can be extremely hard on themselves. Oh, and one last thing: They definitely have the cleanest apartment you've ever seen. (That's a promise.)

STRENGTHS	WEAKNESSES	MOST COMPATIBLE WITH
Hardworking	Judgmental	Taurus
Analytical	Stressed	Capricorn
Methodical	Perfectionist	Cancer
Humble	Controlling	Scorpio
Kind	Rigid	Pisces

VIRGO BINGO

Bookshelves are 100 percent color-coordinated	Buys disinfectant wipes	Most likely to be a student council member	"I'm a little Type A."	Schedules everything down to the minute
Secretly loves making grocery lists	Deep-cleans the entire house	"Let me check my Google Cal."	The freakiest of all control freaks	Probably has a coffee addiction
"The devil's in the details."	(Is the devil in said details)	FREE SPACE to disinfect a surface	"You're doing it wrong..."	Was/is obviously a straight-A student
Identified as a "gifted child"	Googles their symptoms when they feel *at all* under the weather	Panics after self-diagnosis	Self-soothes by reorganizing the fridge	Forgives but never, *ever* forgets
An advocate for clean, sleek designs	Dare I say... minimalist?	Buys more disinfectant wipes	"You missed a spot..."	*Big* fan of Marie Kondo

♎ LIBRA

SEPTEMBER 23–OCTOBER 22

As an air sign, Libras are naturally some of the most charming, kindhearted, and friendliest people of all the zodiac. They are natural peacekeepers and seek harmony in all aspects of their lives, as you'd probably guess, given that their symbol is the scales. They do tend to be people pleasers, but that's only because they see both sides in every argument, and want to make sure everyone feels heard! Libras are also quite the aesthetic people. They usually have a very specific personal style and take pride in their appearance. Basically, Libras are hot as hell!

STRENGTHS	WEAKNESSES	MOST COMPATIBLE WITH
Charming	Codependent	Gemini
Diplomatic	Indecisive	Aquarius
Sociable	Superficial	Leo
Romantic	Judgmental	Sagittarius
Artistic	Easily influenced	Aries

LIBRA BINGO

All about The Aesthetic™	Has an art museum membership	Sees both sides of an argument	Indecisive × 1,000	Their outfits never miss!!!
Tries to mediate every fight	Redecorates bedroom every 2–3 weeks	"To play devil's advocate…"	*Cannot. Keep. A. Secret.*	Highly active on *Pinterest*
Somehow is always at every party???	"They're just jealous of me!"	FREE SPACE for a retail therapy break	Admires their reflection in shop windows	Always texting seven people at once
Has a slight victim complex	Can't yell without crying	Romanticizes everything ever	A true People Pleaser™	*Rose quartz rattles around in bag*
Spends life savings at Sephora	Has a crush on every stranger	"I need a night out!!!"	Craves a tender forehead kiss	Love language aficionado

♏

SCORPIO

OCTOBER 23–NOVEMBER 21

Did someone say "dark, brooding, and incredibly sexy and mysterious"? Yeah, "Scorpio" is the same thing. Often referred to as "the fire sign of the water signs" because of how headstrong and passionate they are, Scorpios have an intense air unlike any of the other signs. Much like their symbol, the scorpion, people born under the sign of Scorpio are deeply devoted lovers, but will easily turn around and sting you if you do them dirty. They're your biggest cheerleader—that is, until you've wronged them. Basically, these scorpions like to lurk in the shadows not because they're shifty, but because that's where they're able to see things as they truly are—no smoke or mirrors.

STRENGTHS	WEAKNESSES	MOST COMPATIBLE WITH
Passionate	Jealous	Cancer
Devoted	Vengeful	Pisces
Emotional	Brooding	Taurus
Loyal	Possessive	Virgo
Protective	Controlling	Capricorn

SCORPIO BINGO

Has an all-black wardrobe	Low-key seduced by the moon???	Uses snakes as a style motif	Holds a grudge	~Full of secrets~
Has *the most* piercing eyes	Grade A Internet creeper	Always told, "You're so intimidating!"	Has a breakdown	Dyes their hair
Ever-expanding healing crystal collection	Halloween, but in human form	FREE SPACE to stare into the void	"Tell me your deepest trauma."	Same energy as a haunted doll
Gets jealous easily (like, *too* easily)	Vengeful, but it's kinda hot...?	Obsessed with all things occult	Angelina-Jolie-while-married-to-Billy-Bob-Thornton energy	"Wanna come to a séance?"
Always looks mad unintentionally	A little *too* into true crime	Withholds information	"I'm a Slytherin."	*Still* holding that grudge

SAGITTARIUS

NOVEMBER 22–DECEMBER 21

If you're looking for the perfect adventure partner, look no further than Sagittarius. This fire sign lives for travel, nights out...basically all things spontaneous and unpredictable! Represented by the archer, Sagittarians are usually funny, life-of-the-party types, but are also known to indulge in a deep, philosophical convo from time to time. They're freethinkers, eternal optimists, and witty conversationalists. Sagittarians love to share their thoughts and ideas with just about anyone they meet along the way, and if you're lucky enough to cross paths with one, you will never forget it.

STRENGTHS	WEAKNESSES	MOST COMPATIBLE WITH
Independent	Noncommittal	Aries
Optimistic	Restless	Leo
Adventurous	Irresponsible	Gemini
Philosophical	Impatient	Libra
Excitable	Naive	Aquarius

SAGITTARIUS BINGO

~wAnDeRlUsT~	"One time, in Cabo…"	Their mind is alarmingly open	Fond of Irish goodbyes	"I need space!!!"
An eternal optimist	A bad driver	EXTROVERT!!!!	Has a travel *Pinterest* board	Will try anything once
Pregame host with the most	Adrenaline junkie	FREE SPACE to wing it	Flirts with everyone	Ghosts everyone
Has no greater fear than FOMO	Self-identifies as a free spirit	Takes a last-minute road trip	The Funny Friend™	"I'm sooooo bored!"
Majorly turned off by clinginess	Thinks they're a philosopher	Searches *Zillow* in different cities	Always laughs at the worst times	Has tons of frequent flyer miles

♑ CAPRICORN

DECEMBER 22–JANUARY 19

When it comes to hard work, the first sign that comes to mind is obviously Capricorn. These lil' sea goats (yup, that's really their symbol) are the epitome of an earth sign—driven, goal-oriented, and 100 percent dedicated to seeing things through, even if it takes years. They're often perceived as serious and standoffish—which they can be—but Capricorns can also be pretty funny, with dry wit and sharp one-liners that could rival those of any Gemini! At their core, Capricorns are highly intellectual people who approach life logically and strategically, and take pride in their competence. Basically, if you need someone in your life who's reliable and responsible, find yourself a Capricorn!

STRENGTHS	WEAKNESSES	MOST COMPATIBLE WITH
Hardworking	Rigid	Taurus
Organized	Greedy	Virgo
Disciplined	Cynical	Cancer
Determined	Stubborn	Scorpio
Intellectual	Workaholic	Pisces

CAPRICORN BINGO

Secretly loves being overworked	Most likely to be a teacher's pet (obviously)	Checks bank account for the 1,000th time	"Can you Venmo me?"	Favorite social media platform is *LinkedIn*
"So I outlined the budget..."	"Your network is your net worth."	Always ten minutes early to everything	So hardworking it's kinda concerning	Cries in the shower
Stoic	Schedules time to "relax"	FREE SPACE to send Venmo request reminders	Took gym class *waaaay* too seriously as a kid	"Why is everyone incompetent?!"
Checks email for the 10,000th time	All about $$$$$$$	Browses job listings for fun	Left-brained	"As per my last email..."
Looooves rules	Hall monitor, but make it hot	Gets promoted... again!	Prides themselves on being "self-made"	STONKS MEME ♥

AQUARIUS

JANUARY 20–FEBRUARY 18

In the best way humanly possible, Aquarians are the weirdos of the zodiac. Even though they're an air sign, they're symbolized by the water bearer (which is kinda confusing, I know). Aquarians pride themselves on being original, artistic, and—let's be honest here—completely visionary. These otherworldly folks hate small talk and would much rather talk philosophy and spirituality, debate ideas, or even decode your dreams. With their free-spirited inclinations, Aquarians can often be hard to pin down, and can even seem a bit detached when it comes to emotions. They tend to romanticize being esoteric and have no problem living in their own little world. In fact, they probably prefer it that way!

STRENGTHS	WEAKNESSES	MOST COMPATIBLE WITH
Artistic	Detached	Aries
Free-spirited	Irresponsible	Leo
Self-reliant	Unreliable	Sagittarius
Nonconformist	Rebellious	Gemini
Visionary	Unemotional	Libra

AQUARIUS BINGO

"OMG, in my dream last night..."	Thinks aliens are definitely real	Clothes never match, but they work...???	Probably went to art school (if they aren't going right now)	Has a mental breakdown
Dyes hair, like, *acid* green	Loves being called "weird"	Hates authority... like, *hates* it	Emotionally detached	Conspiracy theorist by trade
Romanticizes outer space	Indepen-dent... maybe *too* independent	FREE SPACE to astral project	Abhors small talk	"I'm such a loner."
Prides themselves on being "different"	Commit-ment-phobe	The Black Sheep™ of the family	Puts the "culture" in "subculture"	Into taxidermy or something else weird
Clearly not of this world	Gets bored of acid green hair	Dyes hair purple	Probably has a nose ring	Has a stick-and-poke tattoo

PISCES

FEBRUARY 19–MARCH 20

As the last sign of the zodiac, sensitive lil' water sign Pisces feels everything—like, *everything*. Think of Pisceans as emotional sponges: They absorb the energies and feelings of everyone around them. This can be extremely difficult, but when harnessed the right way, Pisceans' emotional intuition is actually more like a superpower. Because of this, Pisceans tend to be drawn to all things spiritual and feel a deep connection to a higher realm. That's why Pisces is symbolized by two fish—one down in the emotional depths, the other in the higher spiritual plane. They're also prone to moodiness, indecision, and sometimes even codependency, as they can often find themselves lacking direction. Yet, when highly evolved, Pisceans are some of the most imaginative, caring, and open-minded people you'll ever meet.

STRENGTHS	WEAKNESSES	MOST COMPATIBLE WITH
Intuitive	Wishy-washy	Cancer
Compassionate	Moody	Scorpio
Spiritual	Codependent	Taurus
Romantic	Overly sensitive	Virgo
Adaptable	Submissive	Capricorn

PISCES BINGO

The Therapist Friend™	Keeps a dream journal	Really into meditation	Charges crystals on a windowsill	Literally *feels* the moon phases
Loves every animal ever	"I won't take it personally!"	...Takes it personally	"I'm an empath."	Romanticizes the little things
Hurts own feelings	Feels everyone's energies at all times	FREE SPACE to daydream	Cries while watching animal videos	Cries while watching any video, really
Stops to smell *every* rose	Artistically gifted	"No worries!"	Has many, *many* worries	"I just have a lot of feelings!"
Suffers for their art	Big ol' savior complex	Falls in love *suuuuper* easily	Has an extensive sad song playlist	*Happy cries*

✳

CHAPTER 2

The Signs and Their Relationships

Sometimes, you need to look outside yourself and your own sign to really understand what makes you who you are—you need to look at the signs of those you attract and are attracted to! What's it like when you're an Aries and you date a Leo, or—*gasp!*—a *Pisces*?! Or what if you're a Scorpio and you're dating a Cancer, but for some reason, you can't keep your mind off that deliriously delectable Sagittarius??? Romantic relationships—whether they be committed, unrequited, or just for fun—really are written in the stars. And, IDK, something about love and destiny being intertwined with the universe is just a little bit... *sexy*?

So, how does *your* sign flirt? Which sign is the most awkward on a first date? How do each of the signs fare during a breakup? What sign are you bound to attract? These are the kinds of burning questions that you will find answered in the following carefully curated charts. May they reveal a lil' sumthin'-sumthin' about the special someone(s) in your life!

The signs trying to flirt

ARIES
Starts bullying you

TAURUS
Is not above a classic Netflix and Chill

GEMINI
Challenges you to a battle of wits

CANCER
Bakes you cookies, or just asks you about your day

LEO
"Wanna come to my show tonight?"

VIRGO
They, like, don't flirt

LIBRA
Invites you to collab on their *Pinterest* board

SCORPIO
Stares at you

SAGITTARIUS
"Let's go on a weekend getaway!"

CAPRICORN
Connects with you on *LinkedIn*

AQUARIUS
Makes a weird painting for you or something

PISCES
Serenades you in a borderline cringey way

The signs and their dating app profiles

ARIES	**TAURUS**	**GEMINI**
Every pic is clearly taken using a ring light	"Swipe right if you have good taste!"	"Don't worry, that baby is my niece."

CANCER	**LEO**	**VIRGO**
Lots of pictures with random children to show that they're "family-oriented"	Mirror pic. Vacation pic. Party pic. Selfie. Another mirror pic.	"Will organize and color-coordinate your entire life for you in exchange for unconditional love."

LIBRA	**SCORPIO**	**SAGITTARIUS**
"Your mom will love me."	Has a pic of them with their ex, but their ex's face is blurred out	Every pic is a group shot, so you never know which one they are

CAPRICORN	**AQUARIUS**	**PISCES**
Their first pic is 1,000 percent their *LinkedIn* photo	"Not looking for anything serious at the moment."	"Just looking for someone I can romanticize and make playlists for."

The signs on first dates

ARIES
Wants to do something wild and exciting!!!

TAURUS
Wants to be spoiled (as they should be!)

GEMINI
Talks a lot to fill awkward silences

CANCER
Brings along their marriage checklist

LEO
Sees a first date as a varsity tryout

VIRGO
Is *extremely* hard to read

LIBRA
Turns up charm to one thousand

SCORPIO
Asks lots of questions, but stays guarded

SAGITTARIUS
Susses you out through light, flirty banter

CAPRICORN
Wants to see credentials up front

AQUARIUS
Plays up their innate, sexy shock value

PISCES
Somehow finds a way to make every little thing profoundly romantic

The signs and the best places

ARIES

AN AMUSEMENT PARK
They'll love the adrenaline
rush of it all

TAURUS

A COZY COFFEE SHOP
They'll love unwinding and opening
up in a warm atmosphere

LEO

THE BEACH
They'll love getting to hang
out in the sun together

VIRGO

A FARMERS' MARKET
They'll love strolling
around and just chatting

SAGITTARIUS

A CONCERT
They'll love spending a fun,
wild night out together

CAPRICORN

AN ARCADE
They'll love getting to be
competitive right off the bat

to take them on a first date

GEMINI

TRIVIA NIGHT
They'll love having a
battle of the minds

CANCER

THE MOVIES
They'll love the classic-
ness of the date

LIBRA

A BOTANICAL GARDEN
Being surrounded by beauty
will help them open up

SCORPIO

**A LESSER-KNOWN HOLE-IN-
THE-WALL RESTAURANT**
They'll love the element of mystery

AQUARIUS

A PLANETARIUM
They'll love getting to zone
out...with someone special!

PISCES

A PICNIC
They'll love getting to be all
cutesy in the outdoors

The signs meeting the parents

ARIES

Brings a gift as a preemptive peace offering

TAURUS

Bakes something to win the folks over

GEMINI

Fills every awkward silence with nervous rambling

CANCER

Finds similarities between themselves and the parents to be rather Freudian

LEO

Makes a point to show off one—if not more—of their many talents

VIRGO

Engages one of the parents in an intellectual convo right off the bat

LIBRA

Asks to see baby photos *immediately*

SCORPIO

Interrogates parents about their kid, but in a ~charming~ way

SAGITTARIUS

Is so friendly to the parents that it reads as borderline flirting

CAPRICORN

Offers to help with every last task

AQUARIUS

"Your child is very weird, but just the right kind of weird."

PISCES

Brings a giant, sappy bouquet of flowers

The signs during breakups

ARIES

Makes a dart board with their ex's face on it

TAURUS

Cries while baking a loaf of bread and eats the entire thing in one sitting

GEMINI

Angrily subtweets their ex

CANCER

Cries. For *years*.

LEO

Uses heartbreak as motivation to get hotter

VIRGO

Rearranges their bedroom while crying

LIBRA

Wants to cry, but doesn't feel like ruining their makeup

SCORPIO

Harbors a deep resentment for their ex forever, that's all!

SAGITTARIUS

Redownloads dating apps STAT

CAPRICORN

Immediately channels energy into something else (work)

AQUARIUS

Goes on a solo camping trip to "reconnect with nature"

PISCES

Falls apart, and then makes art about it

The signs and the sign they always

ARIES

SCORPIO

TAURUS

LEO

LEO

VIRGO

VIRGO

PISCES

SAGITTARIUS

CAPRICORN

CAPRICORN

AQUARIUS

seem to attract for some reason...?

GEMINI	CANCER
CANCER	SAGITTARIUS

LIBRA	SCORPIO
ARIES	LIBRA

AQUARIUS	PISCES
TAURUS	GEMINI

The signs and what makes them fall in love

ARIES	TAURUS	GEMINI
Being direct and knowing what you want	Smelling really, *really* good	Always having a good comeback

CANCER	LEO	VIRGO
Being a great listener	Being more powerful than they are	Stimulating, intellectual conversation

LIBRA	SCORPIO	SAGITTARIUS
A good debate	Dominant personalities	When someone is down for anything

CAPRICORN	AQUARIUS	PISCES
Having your life "together"	Resisting authority	Deep, emotional heart-to-hearts

The signs and what will make them fall out of love

ARIES

Being "too available"

TAURUS

Being generally chaotic

GEMINI

Routine

CANCER

Having a big ego

LEO

Negative attitudes

VIRGO

Unhygienic, unmotivated, lazy ol' slobs!!!

LIBRA

Starting drama for literally no reason

SCORPIO

Liars!!!

SAGITTARIUS

Being controlled

CAPRICORN

Being unjustly arrogant

AQUARIUS

Clinginess

PISCES

Being dismissive and close-minded

ARIES

VEGAS WEDDING
Spontaneous, to-the-point, and
all about you and your love

TAURUS

FOREST WEDDING
Lush, dreamlike, and
rooted in the outdoors

LEO

OUTDOOR WEDDING WITH FIREWORKS
Loud, flashy, and memorable

VIRGO

ALL-WHITE WEDDING
Simple, clean, and timeless

SAGITTARIUS

DESTINATION WEDDING IN THE JUNGLE
Invigorating, wild, and uninhibited

CAPRICORN

WINTER WEDDING
Elegant, refined, and luxurious

their dream weddings

GEMINI

BEACH WEDDING
Freeing, fun for all, and
party-centric

CANCER

BACKYARD WEDDING
Family-oriented, sentimental,
and nostalgic

LIBRA

GARDEN PARTY WEDDING
Light, airy, and undeniably beautiful

SCORPIO

FALL WEDDING
Gothic, candlelit, and cozy

AQUARIUS

CITY HALL WEDDING
Unconventional, quick, and personal

PISCES

CASTLE WEDDING
Romantic, magical, and
straight out of a fairytale

The signs and their own red flag habits

ARIES	TAURUS	GEMINI
Gets angry *waaay* too quickly	Unfathomably stubborn and lazy	Spreads rumors like the flu
CANCER	**LEO**	**VIRGO**
Emotionally manipulative	Somehow always makes everything about them	So judgmental that sometimes it's just, like, enough already!
LIBRA	**SCORPIO**	**SAGITTARIUS**
Soooo indecisive, it's almost criminal	Literally just plain sinister	Can't commit to anyone or anything
CAPRICORN	**AQUARIUS**	**PISCES**
Incredibly uptight and rigid	So unconventional that it can be alienating	Just an emotional mess—no other way to put it

The signs and their soul mates

ARIES

Someone who doesn't try to control them, and is instead charmed and amused by them

TAURUS

Someone secure and stable who will enjoy the finer things in life with them

GEMINI

Someone who could listen to them talk forever and still follow up with leading questions

CANCER

Someone who puts them first and takes care of them for a change

LEO

Someone who worships the ground they walk on, and is equally impressive on their own

VIRGO

Someone practical, but who also helps them unwind a little bit

LIBRA

Someone with both beauty and brains

SCORPIO

Someone loyal who won't shy away from deep, emotional conversations

SAGITTARIUS

Someone who is more than willing to tag along on their adventures

CAPRICORN

Someone who will comfort them and teach them how to stop and smell the roses

AQUARIUS

Someone intellectual and captivating who will always support their creative endeavors

PISCES

Someone who will ground them and constantly reassure them of their feelings

The signs and their

ARIES

PHUKET, THAILAND
Visit an elephant sanctuary
and waterfalls, and
contemplate Buddhism

TAURUS

FLORENCE, ITALY
Indulge in food, cappuccinos,
culture, and romantic moped rides

LEO

SANTORINI, GREECE
Photos of them and their partner
in white linen guaranteed

VIRGO

TOKYO, JAPAN
Visit temples and go on bike
rides through cherry blossoms

SAGITTARIUS

BORANA, KENYA
Safaris, skydiving, and lots
of make-out seshes

CAPRICORN

BRITISH COLUMBIA, CANADA
Explore national parks and
cozy up in a luxury cabin

dream honeymoons

GEMINI

BORA BORA, FRENCH POLYNESIA
Stay in an overwater bungalow
and drink out of coconuts

CANCER

MAJORCA, SPAIN
Explore limestone caves and
float in the Balearic Sea

LIBRA

PARIS, FRANCE
Spend lots of time
canoodling in cafés

SCORPIO

PRAGUE, CZECH REPUBLIC
Go on castle tours, NBD

AQUARIUS

CINQUE TERRE, ITALY
Go completely off the grid
in a cliffside village

PISCES

KAUAI, HAWAII
Hike by day, treat selves
to a spa by night

CHAPTER 3

The Signs and Their Families

Something people often overlook in astrology is the importance of family. Sure, you're an Aquarius, but how does that change things if your mom is a Cancer? Or what if ALL. FOUR. OF. YOUR. SIBLINGS. ARE. TAUREANS?! (Hey, it can happen!) Looking at the different signs in your family tree will not only help you better understand your fam and where you fit into these dynamics, but more likely than not, you'll notice sign patterns. Let's just say: If you're a Sagittarius, you had to have gotten that Sag from somewhere!

Still, each sign has its own unique way of operating within a family, and, for your reading/memeing pleasure, they're all laid out in this chapter. How would *your* sign act at a family reunion? Or when hanging out with your partner's parents? Everyone has at least one weird relative they have blocked on social media— which one does your sign have it out for? Family is sweet, stressful, loving, annoying, and just about every other descriptor one can think of. They also come in all different shapes, sizes, and—you guessed it—signs. Let's see what the stars say about you and your family!

The signs posing for a family photo

ARIES

Puts their arm around their sibling who they were screaming at five minutes ago

TAURUS

Makes sure to stand so the camera is getting their good side

GEMINI

Tries to be "funny" and gives someone bunny ears

CANCER

Forces everyone to say "Cheese!" as the photo is being taken

LEO

Stands front and center, of course!!!

VIRGO

Asks to see the picture after it's taken to make sure they look good

LIBRA

Points out the best background for the shot

SCORPIO

Glares at the camera

SAGITTARIUS

Intentionally ruins the shot by making a weird face

CAPRICORN

Insists on taking the picture so they don't have to be in it

AQUARIUS

Commence groaning

PISCES

Sneezes

ARIES

The bossy, know-it-all, high achiever sibling

TAURUS

The sibling who lives in their parents' basement

LEO

The funny, charming sibling who gets all the attention

VIRGO

The quiet sibling who just kinda sits back and observes

SAGITTARIUS

The sibling who's always injured for some reason...?

CAPRICORN

The sibling who is a boss both academically *and* athletically

as siblings

GEMINI

The notorious tattletale sibling

CANCER

The sibling who cries in their room to piano ballads

LIBRA

The sibling who always acts as the family mediator

SCORPIO

The plotting sibling the parents think can do no wrong

AQUARIUS

The sibling often described as "the black sheep" or "oddball"

PISCES

The sibling who's always lost in a daydream

The signs on a family vacation

ARIES
Forgets passport

TAURUS
Overpacks by a whole suitcase

GEMINI
Doesn't stop talking the whole way there

CANCER
"Can we all just get along for once?!"

LEO
Can be found flirting with people at the hotel bar

VIRGO
Schedules trip itinerary down to the minute

LIBRA
Makes their sibling take hot Instas of them

SCORPIO
Wanders off on their own; not seen for another twelve hours

SAGITTARIUS
Wants to try every adventure and activity available

CAPRICORN
Triple-checks every restaurant bill

AQUARIUS
Casually builds the most impressive sandcastle anyone's ever seen

PISCES
Plays mermaids in the pool all day with the kids and *loves* it

The signs at family reunions

ARIES
Starts a fight with a cousin over politics

TAURUS
Loiters around the appetizers

GEMINI
Gets roped into talking to the weird uncle

CANCER
"I haven't seen you since you were a little baby!"

LEO
Tries to one-up every semi-successful relative

VIRGO
Made matching family reunion T-shirts for everyone

LIBRA
"Do I seriously have to wear this family reunion T-shirt?"

SCORPIO
Stands in the back and just watches things unfold

SAGITTARIUS
Is the weird uncle

CAPRICORN
Planned and organized every last bonding activity down to a *T*

AQUARIUS
Mysteriously disappears and shows up again hours later with no explanation

PISCES
Reminisces with the elderly relatives

The signs and the one childhood

ARIES

Their stuffed animal that went *everywhere* with them

TAURUS

Their super soft and snuggly blankie

LEO

Their first onesie with lil' stars on it

VIRGO

Their tiny, tiny T-shirt they used to wear all the time

SAGITTARIUS

Their first pair of baby shoes

CAPRICORN

Their first school project that warranted an A+

belonging their mom just can't get rid of

GEMINI

Their favorite doll they used to talk to for *hours*

CANCER

Their favorite bedtime story

LIBRA

A drawing they did of their beloved childhood pet

SCORPIO

Their first Halloween costume

AQUARIUS

A lock of their hair saved from a self-inflicted "haircut"

PISCES

Their first masterpiece...of many

The signs and their favorite distant relatives

ARIES

That one suggested DNA match who tried to connect with them on Ancestry.com

TAURUS

The perpetually grumpy great-grandma

GEMINI

Their mom's friend who they call their "aunt" but there's actually no blood relation whatsoever

CANCER

The dog at the reunion

LEO

Some uncle's much, much younger girlfriend

VIRGO

The great-great(?)-grandpa who makes everything about "the war"

LIBRA

The latest baby

SCORPIO

The uncle who everyone knows is a philandering lawyer but nobody will say it

SAGITTARIUS

The cool, rich aunt who never had kids and wears all black

CAPRICORN

The great-aunt who always gives them cards with money in them

AQUARIUS

The angsty teen who is clearly going through it and makes it everyone else's problem

PISCES

The great-aunt who's neck-deep in a pyramid scheme

The signs and the one weird relative they have blocked on social media

ARIES	TAURUS	GEMINI
Their super political uncle who always needs to have the last word	Their cousin who's made being engaged her entire personality	Their estranged uncle who is 1,000 percent a flat-earther

CANCER	LEO	VIRGO
Their second cousin who posts about every little thing her toddler does	Their mom because what she doesn't know won't kill her!	Their in-law who is deeply involved in an MLM

LIBRA	SCORPIO	SAGITTARIUS
Their bronzed aunt who has semi-recently become a bodybuilder	Their second cousin who doesn't know who Cher is	Their aunt who tags them 100,000,000 times a day in different comments

CAPRICORN	AQUARIUS	PISCES
Their uncle who shares news articles not knowing they're satire	Their uncle who always comments on their pictures in a debatably creepy way	Their cousin who's a freelance writer and shares every last think piece they publish

ARIES

A medal from World War I

TAURUS

Grandma's high school yearbook from back in the day

LEO

Their great-great-grandma's hand mirror

VIRGO

A passed-down book on their family genealogy

SAGITTARIUS

An old map from when their ancestors immigrated

CAPRICORN

Their great-grandpa's briefcase

family heirlooms

GEMINI

An old newspaper clipping
about their family

CANCER

Their great-grandma's
engagement ring

LIBRA

Their mom's wedding dress

SCORPIO

Their great-aunt's secret diary

AQUARIUS

A painting by an especially
eccentric ancestor

PISCES

Love letters between their
grandparents

The signs as parents

ARIES
Coaches all of the kids' sports teams with *enthusiasm*

TAURUS
Gives the best goodnight hugs

GEMINI
Always drowning in PTA meetings and bake sales

CANCER
"Did you remember your homework? What about your lunch?!"

LEO
Secretly wants to be a momager

VIRGO
Finds packing the kids' lunches oddly satisfying...???

LIBRA
Goes overboard buying all the cutest kids' clothes

SCORPIO
Will fight any teacher who poorly grades their kids

SAGITTARIUS
Tells the most imaginative bedtime stories

CAPRICORN
Looks over their kids' report cards concernedly

AQUARIUS
Hangs every drawing their kids do up on the fridge

PISCES
Keeps a box of all the things their kids make

The signs and their partner's family

ARIES
Sizes up their partner's dad

TAURUS
Hangs out with their partner's siblings without their partner

GEMINI
Calls their partner's grandma just to chat

CANCER
Has an unspoken rivalry with their partner's mom over who is more nurturing

LEO
Does absolutely everything in their power to get their partner's family to like them... *everything*!!!

VIRGO
Retreats into their shell as their partner's family enters the room

LIBRA
Is low-key attracted to one of their partner's extended relatives, but would *never* admit it

SCORPIO
Is still annoyed at one of their partner's aunts over something they said three years ago

SAGITTARIUS
Swaps travel stories with their partner's cool sibling

CAPRICORN
Is included in their partner's family group chat

AQUARIUS
Has mastered the art of small talk with their partner's family

PISCES
Is more bonded with their partner's mom than they are with their partner

The signs and the gifts their family members give

ARIES

An embarrassingly ironic
graphic T-shirt

TAURUS

Tacky home decor

LEO

Any sort of hand-me-down with
"sentimental value"

VIRGO

Kitchen organizers that don't
work with their personal system

SAGITTARIUS

Merch of a band they loved
last year

CAPRICORN

A nauseatingly sweet-
smelling candle

them that they pretend to love, but secretly hate

GEMINI

Any sort of novelty mug

CANCER

A book they've already read (twice)

LIBRA

A shirt that's just so *not* their style

SCORPIO

A box of chocolates with one missing because someone "just couldn't resist."

AQUARIUS

A plant they very well know they can't care for

PISCES

A DVD of a movie they can easily stream

The signs going home for the holidays

ARIES

Rehearses their argument points for any hypothetical family debate that may arise

TAURUS

Is most excited to see their family dog

GEMINI

Looks forward to gossiping with their cousins above all else

CANCER

Tries to get everyone to do cliché holiday activities

LEO

Hits up all their hometown friends to hang out

VIRGO

Plans holiday dinner outfits a month in advance

LIBRA

Packs four (*four!*) suitcases for a 4–6-day trip

SCORPIO

Purposefully hides from any and all hometown acquaintances

SAGITTARIUS

Holiday shops last-minute

CAPRICORN

Willingly plows snow out of the driveway

AQUARIUS

Audibly groans at the concept of doing any remotely cliché holiday activity

PISCES

Surprises everyone by bringing home their new beau of two weeks

CHAPTER 4

The Signs and Their Friends

A *ah,* friendship. One of the greatest blessings we get in this life! Having people to laugh with, lean on, and just spend time with (perhaps you're even skimming through this book with them right now!) is literally *everything.* But have you ever considered how being a Leo might affect the friendships you have? Or how you and your besties' signs complement one another?

This chapter will help you look at yourself and your friends, and uncover the ways in which you're different—and the ways in which you're basically twins. What role does your sign typically take on in the friend group? What are your friends most likely to reply in the group chat? (Hint: Don't expect a rare, one-word contribution from Gemini.) And which signs are destined to be your best friends forever?! Through the following charts, you'll see your friends in a new astrological light, and remember that important, lifelong connections can be made between any signs—it's just about how you nurture them! The next time you and your friends are all together, consider flipping back to these pages. You might be surprised to learn a thing or two about each other, or at least have a funny conversation about whether you'd actually say XYZ in your group chat.

The signs in their friend groups

ARIES
The one who has the most entertaining dating life

TAURUS
The one who everyone else always goes to for advice

GEMINI
The one who knows all the dirt on everyone else

CANCER
The one who always checks in on everyone

LEO
The one who always suggests going out

VIRGO
The one who cleans up everyone else's messes (both figuratively and literally)

LIBRA
The one who tries to mediate all the drama

SCORPIO
The one who sits back and watches all the drama (that they started)

SAGITTARIUS
The one who always has tickets to "that cool thing"

CAPRICORN
The one who divides up the check at brunch

AQUARIUS
The one who makes everyone go to their art show

PISCES
The one who cries on nights out

The signs as

ARIES

The post–pillow fight pillow that's seen better days

TAURUS

The sturdy home base (a.k.a. the pillow fort)

LEO

The bottle of nail polish, of course

VIRGO

The rousing game of M.A.S.H.

SAGITTARIUS

The homemade pizza

CAPRICORN

The gooey s'mores

sleepover necessities

GEMINI

The big ol' bowl of popcorn

CANCER

The jumbo bag of candy

LIBRA

The DVD copy of *Dirty Dancing*

SCORPIO

The Ouija board that scares the crap out of everyone

AQUARIUS

The chaotically collaged vision boards

PISCES

The cooling cucumber face masks

The signs on a night out

ARIES
Befriends every stranger in the bathroom

TAURUS
"It's 9 p.m....it's getting late!"

GEMINI
Goes up to the DJ and requests a different song every 5–7 minutes

CANCER
Makes sure you all get a cute group pic

LEO
Dances in the DJ booth

VIRGO
"I like the ambience here..."

LIBRA
Feverishly documents the entire night on *Instagram*

SCORPIO
Makes eyes at every sexy stranger

SAGITTARIUS
Flirts with everyone, and gets free stuff for the table

CAPRICORN
"Everyone here seems so cool and important!"

AQUARIUS
"I got the address of the after-party!"

PISCES
Tries to make out with everyone

The signs and how their friends would describe them

ARIES
Enthusiastic, supportive, and loyal

TAURUS
Kind, honest, and dependable

GEMINI
Hilarious, exhilarating, and in-the-know

CANCER
Nurturing, welcoming, and empathetic

LEO
Dramatic, entertaining, and big-hearted

VIRGO
Logical, humble, and witty

LIBRA
Fun, caring, and gives good advice

SCORPIO
Protective, trustworthy, and ambitious

SAGITTARIUS
Goofy, clever, and down for anything

CAPRICORN
Rational, dedicated, and wise

AQUARIUS
Unapologetic, creative, and free-spirited

PISCES
Authentic, loving, and imaginative

The signs and their

ARIES

Some ol' faithful eggs Benedict

TAURUS

A stack of pancakes slathered in butter and syrup

LEO

Avocado toast, naturally

VIRGO

A latte with the most elaborate foam art you've ever seen in your *life*

SAGITTARIUS

A bagel with all the fixin's (lox, cream cheese, capers, tomato, and red onion)

CAPRICORN

A steaming cup of black coffee

go-to brunch orders

GEMINI

Literally just an entire plate of hash browns

CANCER

French toast sprinkled with powdered sugar

LIBRA

A highly *Instagram*-able açai bowl

SCORPIO

Deviled eggs with extra devil (a.k.a. hot sauce)

AQUARIUS

A hot skillet of spicy huevos rancheros

PISCES

Some decadent Belgian waffles (beautifully accented with strawberries)

The signs in a group chat

ARIES

Sends a selfie "Is this cute to post on Insta?!"

TAURUS

Sporadically reacts to messages with a "love" or "haha"

GEMINI

Screenshots another convo and drops it in the group chat for deliberation

CANCER

Typically says wholesome things like, "Hope everyone has a great day!"

LEO

Always tries to coordinate a night out

VIRGO

Polls everyone on which outfit they should wear on a first date

LIBRA

Asks for relationship advice every 2–3 weeks

SCORPIO

Their main contribution is screenshots of their Tinder matches' profiles

SAGITTARIUS

Sends a funny TikTok every so often

CAPRICORN

"OMG my coworker is incompetent."

AQUARIUS

Sends an obscure meme that no one truly understands

PISCES

"Does anyone know if Mercury's retrograde?!"

The signs on video chat

ARIES
Will talk for approximately two minutes before getting distracted by something else

TAURUS
Exclusively takes calls while on the toilet

GEMINI
Calls friends multiple times a day to talk about nothing

CANCER
Only calls when someone needs advice or they themselves are in crisis

LEO
Stares at themselves on the screen the whole time

VIRGO
Productively completes a million little tasks while on the call

LIBRA
"OMG I look so ugly right now! Don't look!!!"

SCORPIO
Ignores the call

SAGITTARIUS
Calls you from a random rooftop party and you can't hear anything they say

CAPRICORN
Ignores the call and sends back one of the automated rejection messages

AQUARIUS
Films themselves from a particularly unflattering angle

PISCES
Films themselves from a particularly unflattering angle, but they somehow still look good

ARIES

Blasts loud music when they're angry

TAURUS

Prone to leaving dirty dishes in the sink

LEO

Takes the longest getting ready in the bathroom

VIRGO

Takes it upon themselves to implement a chore chart

SAGITTARIUS

Always has friends over

CAPRICORN

Advocates for a roommate board game night

as roommates

GEMINI

Shares every detail of their day when they get home

CANCER

Bakes a lot and always shares

LIBRA

Redecorates the living room just because

SCORPIO

Hides in their bedroom

AQUARIUS

Always cooks the most unheard of—and delicious—recipes

PISCES

Waters everyone's plants because they know they'll forget

The signs and their BFF signs

ARIES
GEMINI

Aries keeps Gemini motivated, and Gemini stimulates Aries with their intellectual convos

TAURUS
CANCER

Taurus helps Cancer advocate for themselves, and Cancer softens Taurus' stubbornness

GEMINI
ARIES

Gemini encourages Aries to talk through their emotions, and Aries holds Gemini accountable for their actions

CANCER
TAURUS

Cancer helps Taurus acknowledge their feelings, and Taurus cheers on Cancer through their self-doubt

LEO
LIBRA

Libra inspires Leo creatively, and Leo encourages Libra to step into their power

VIRGO
CAPRICORN

Virgo values Capricorn's strong work ethic, and Capricorn admires Virgo's attention to detail

LIBRA
LEO

Libra keeps Leo mindful of others, and Leo always supports Libra's social endeavors

SCORPIO
PISCES

Scorpio validates Pisces' sensitive nature, and Pisces softens Scorpio's cold exterior

SAGITTARIUS
AQUARIUS

Sagittarius is drawn to Aquarius' philosophical mind, and Aquarius feels at home with Sagittarius' spontaneity

CAPRICORN
VIRGO

Capricorn trusts Virgo's opinions, and Virgo knows Capricorn will always tell them the truth

AQUARIUS
SAGITTARIUS

Aquarius encourages Sagittarius' childlike weirdness, and Sagittarius exposes Aquarius to new, wild experiences

PISCES
SCORPIO

Pisces helps Scorpio stop and smell the roses, and Scorpio makes Pisces stand their ground

The signs and their friends' favorite stories to tell about them

ARIES
When they cursed someone out for accidentally spilling their drink on them

TAURUS
When they broke their arm rolling out of bed

GEMINI
When they talked a bouncer into letting them into a highly exclusive nightclub

CANCER
When they cried during their significant other's cousin's wedding (and they'd never met the cousin before)

LEO
When they made everyone go to a karaoke bar just to listen to them sing

VIRGO
When they spent two straight days organizing all their books into alphabetical order

LIBRA
When they got into a fight over whether a color was "white" or "eggshell"

SCORPIO
When they hexed their ex, and the next day, their ex lost their job

SAGITTARIUS
When they booked a one-way flight to Indonesia and ended up staying for two years

CAPRICORN
When they convinced their boss to give them a raise "just because"

AQUARIUS
When they seduced a C-list celebrity and wouldn't let *anyone* forget it

PISCES
When they predicted when their niece would be born down to the *minute*

The signs and what they'd

ARIES

Some apple cider they picked up from the supermarket on their way over

TAURUS

Mashed potatoes

LEO

Bread rolls that have the perfect fluffy-to-buttery ratio

VIRGO

The whole turkey because they don't trust anyone else to cook it right

SAGITTARIUS

Cranberry sauce

CAPRICORN

Their famous homemade pumpkin pie

bring to friendsgiving

GEMINI

The salad that nobody touches

CANCER

Brownies that they always say are "made with love"

LIBRA

A highly impressive—and artistic—charcuterie board

SCORPIO

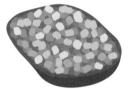

Stuffing!!!

AQUARIUS

Their "mystery" gravy...???

PISCES

Yams that no one touches (and they take that personally)

The signs and their dream bachelor/bachelorette parties

ARIES

Clubbing, clubbing, and, oh yeah...*more clubbing!!!*

TAURUS

Just some good food, good company, and a cozy cabin upstate

GEMINI

I don't even know, but mark my words: There will be purple wigs involved

CANCER

Finding a nice mountainside Airbnb for the weekend and hanging out by a bonfire

LEO

A brunch where they get to wear the classic tiara and "BRIDE" sash combo

VIRGO

Something that revolves around a *very* carefully planned itinerary

LIBRA

VEGAS, BABY!!!!!!!

SCORPIO

A haunted ghost tour through New Orleans

SAGITTARIUS

Two words: PARTY. BUS.

CAPRICORN

Lounging on a beach somewhere warm (preferably in a cabana)

AQUARIUS

A spiritual jungle getaway led by a shaman

PISCES

A spa weekend for proper premarital pampering

*

CHAPTER 5

The Signs and Their Pets

Haven't you always wondered what kind of dog you'd be as a Gemini? Or what kind of cat is *so* Aquarius? Or maybe you're into less run-of-the-mill pets, like bearded dragons, or, like, hermit crabs, and so you wonder what kind of unconventional, semidomesticated creature you'd be as an Aries? Regardless, this chapter is all about your furry, feathered, scaly, four-legged, two-legged, tri-pawed friends and how you love them!

The following charts will reveal answers to all of those questions, as well as stuff like how your sign talks to your pets, which pet toys your sign always buys (even though you already have *waaaaaay* too many), and even what nicknames you're most likely to use. Pets are right up there with friends and family, because, I mean, they *are* family! And astrologically speaking, your pets are just as celestially aligned as you are. With that being said, let's get into it: What kind of Pet Pawrent™ are you—or will be one day—according to the stars?

The signs and the nicknames they give their pets

ARIES
Choochie.
Bean.
Rat.

TAURUS
Bubz.
Tookie.
Snugawump.

GEMINI
Meanie Bobini.
Lover baby.
Snicklefritz.

CANCER
Toot.
Boopers.
Angel baby.

LEO
Sugar booger.
Lovey loo.
Chonker.

VIRGO
Honey bunny.
Chicky pop.
Nooner.

LIBRA
Bubba.
Floof.
Poopy baby.

SCORPIO
Gooby booby.
Baba.
Ma'am/Sir.

SAGITTARIUS
Stink.
Tiny baby.
Fluffernutter.

CAPRICORN
Nugget.
Loaf.
Nug-loaf.

AQUARIUS
Fart fart.
Snooter.
Coo coo bird.

PISCES
Lee lee.
Choochabutt.
Bananie.

ARIES

PUG
Cute and alert; their bark is bigger than their bite

TAURUS

ENGLISH BULLDOG
Loyal, lazy, and highly food-motivated

LEO

POMERANIAN
Small, but big alpha energy

VIRGO

ENGLISH POINTER
Helpful, hardworking, and smart

SAGITTARIUS

AUSTRALIAN SHEPHERD
Adventurous, affectionate, and intelligent

CAPRICORN

GERMAN SHEPHERD
Strong, dutiful, and determined

as dogs

GEMINI

BEAGLE
Social, playful, and vocal

CANCER

LABRADOR RETRIEVER
Loving, supportive, and unwavering

LIBRA

GOLDEN RETRIEVER
Sweet, kind, and objectively
good-looking

SCORPIO

SHIBA INU
Mischievous, strong-
willed, and suspicious

AQUARIUS

CHINESE CRESTED DOG
Different, wacky, and independent

PISCES

BASSET HOUND
Friendly, worried, and patient

The signs talking to their pets

ARIES

"You're a stinky lil' sewer rat!!!" (But means it cutely.)

TAURUS

Speaks to them exclusively in a cockney accent

GEMINI

Baby voice activates

CANCER

Their voice goes up five octaves

LEO

"You're a little bean that fell out of a burrito, aren't you?!"

VIRGO

Asks their pet their opinion on ~various matters~

LIBRA

"You're a wittle baby with a wittle baby booty!!!"

SCORPIO

"Give me kissies or I'll simply have to squish you!!!"

SAGITTARIUS

Communicates in squeaks and other unintelligible noises

CAPRICORN

Speaks to their pet as if they were their business associate

AQUARIUS

Invents a language that only they and their pet understand

PISCES

Sings everything to them. Like, *everything.*

The signs and their pet's favorite spot to sleep

ARIES
Curled up with their head on their owner's shoulder

TAURUS
In their little bed right next to the heater

GEMINI
In a fruit bowl

CANCER
Perched up next to a window

LEO
Unapologetically sprawled out on the couch

VIRGO
In the open sock drawer

LIBRA
On the floor in the little patch of sun

SCORPIO
In the shade under the patio table

SAGITTARIUS
In a pot out in the garden

CAPRICORN
Under the desk in the study

AQUARIUS
In the bathroom sink

PISCES
On their owner's feet

ARIES

SCOTTISH FOLD
Playful, curious, and snuggly

TAURUS

BRITISH SHORTHAIR
Easygoing, docile, and chill

LEO

MAINE COON
Fierce, prepared, and eye-catching

VIRGO

RUSSIAN BLUE
Gentle, quiet, and reserved

SAGITTARIUS

BENGAL
Untamed, unique, and uninhibited

CAPRICORN

MANX
Self-reliant, bright, and elusive

as cats

GEMINI

SIAMESE
Rare, beautiful, and knows
something you don't

CANCER

MUNCHKIN
Affectionate, fun-seeking,
and adorable

LIBRA

PERSIAN
Glamorous, sought-after,
and unbothered

SCORPIO

BLACK
Slinky, superstitious, and mystical

AQUARIUS

SPHYNX
Nonconforming,
fashionable, and freaky

PISCES

RAGDOLL
Sweet, cuddly, and sentimental

The signs and the type of pet pawrent they are

ARIES

The kind whose holiday card is just pictures of them and their pet

TAURUS

The kind who spends their entire life savings on sweaters for their pet

GEMINI

The kind who will 1,000 percent have their pet in their wedding

CANCER

The kind who carries their pet around in a BabyBjörn

LEO

The kind who makes their pet an *Instagram* account (and it has 10,000+ followers)

VIRGO

The kind who has a portrait of their pet hung up in their house

LIBRA

The kind who dresses their pet up in baby onesies

SCORPIO

The kind who sneaks their pet tiny food scraps under the table

SAGITTARIUS

The kind who takes their pet on all sorts of hikes and adventures

CAPRICORN

The kind who organizes the local breed meetups

AQUARIUS

The kind who pushes their pet around in a stroller

PISCES

The kind who lets their pet sleep under the covers with them

The signs taking their pets on a walk

ARIES

Gets slightly annoyed when people stop them to say hi to their pet

TAURUS

Gets offended whenever someone *doesn't* stop them to say hi to their pet

GEMINI

Somehow keeps getting tangled up in their pet's leash...?

CANCER

Stops every two feet to take another picture of their pet

LEO

Always makes sure their pet has the cutest (and most *Instagram*-able) coat on

VIRGO

Puts lil' booties on their pet's paws to protect their lil' feetsies

LIBRA

Walks their pet to Starbucks and gets them a pup cup

SCORPIO

Turns beet red while picking up their pet's poop in front of a hot stranger

SAGITTARIUS

Opts for a long hike with their pet over the standard lap around the block

CAPRICORN

Tracks their pet's steps on a fitness tracker

AQUARIUS

Yells "Leave it!" whenever they and their pet pass a particularly tasty-looking rock

PISCES

Always takes their pet on The Scenic Route™

The signs as

ARIES

GUINEA PIG
Energetic, lovable, and active

TAURUS

TURTLE
Slooooooow, yet steady

LEO

CHINCHILLA
Lively, affectionate, and sociable

VIRGO

HEDGEHOG
Bashful, sweet, and particular

SAGITTARIUS

FENNEC FOX
Curious, charming, and
nature-loving

CAPRICORN

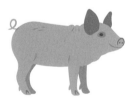

PIG
Smart, independent,
and rambunctious

unconventional pets

GEMINI

NAKED MOLE RAT
Funny, vocal, and bizarre

CANCER

RED FOX
Timid, caring, and quick

LIBRA

ALPACA
Mellow, friendly, and
enjoys company

SCORPIO

SNAKE
Quiet, enigmatic, and self-sufficient

AQUARIUS

FERRET
Spunky, entertaining, and cute

PISCES

AXOLOTL
Precious, shy, and loving

The signs as famous pets

ARIES
Diddy Kong the Marmoset

TAURUS
Doug the Pug

GEMINI
Venus the Two-Faced Cat

CANCER
Lionel the 'Hog

LEO
Jiff Pom

VIRGO
Esther the Wonder Pig

LIBRA
Nala Cat

SCORPIO
Pumpkin the Raccoon

SAGITTARIUS
Juniper Fox

CAPRICORN
Grumpy Cat

AQUARIUS
Tuna the Chiweenie

PISCES
Marnie the Dog

The signs and what they dress their pets up in

ARIES Tie-dyed onesie	**TAURUS** Chunky knit sweater	**GEMINI** Tutu
CANCER T-shirt that says "I ♥ MY PAWRENTS"	**LEO** Hot pink puffer coat	**VIRGO** Overalls
LIBRA Letterman jacket	**SCORPIO** Rainbow-colored onesie	**SAGITTARIUS** Gray hoodie
CAPRICORN Tuxedo	**AQUARIUS** UPS deliveryperson costume	**PISCES** Raincoat

The signs and the pet toys they always buy

ARIES

EXTRA-DURABLE CHEW TOY
Loves to get their aggression out

TAURUS

STUFFED ANIMAL
Very good for both
attacking and cuddling

LEO

CHUCKIT!
Gets to show off their
undeniable athleticism

VIRGO

INTERACTIVE TOY
Loves a good old-fashioned
mind game!!!

SAGITTARIUS

KONG WITH PEANUT BUTTER IN IT
Loves a good challenge

CAPRICORN

TREAT DISPENSER
Loves a treat, but also
loves working for it

(even though they have *waaaaay* too many)

GEMINI

TENNIS BALL
Excitingly off-the-walls

CANCER

FRISBEE
An all-around crowd-pleaser!!!

LIBRA

CHAMPAGNE PLUSH TOY
Classy, but still in on the joke

SCORPIO

CAT SCRATCHER
Tactile and addictive

AQUARIUS

CAT TUNNELS
Simply thrilling

PISCES

LICK MAT
Scrumptious, yet meditative

ARIES

Bold and distinguished leather

TAURUS

Cow print

LEO

Pink and ~bedazzled~

VIRGO

Classy plaid

SAGITTARIUS

Literally just a gold chain with a
name tag

CAPRICORN

Red, with a little bowtie
attached

their pets' collars

GEMINI

Very sassy cheetah print

CANCER

Chevron

LIBRA

Floral print (namely daisies)

SCORPIO

Spooky, with cute little ghosts

AQUARIUS

Rainbow tie-dye

PISCES

Wraparound waves

The signs as dogs at the dog park

ARIES
The one who's irrevocably obsessed with fetch

TAURUS
The one basking in the sun

GEMINI
The one howling at every new dog who enters the park

CANCER
The one who just sleeps on their owner's lap the whole time

LEO
The one who greets every last person and dog at the park

VIRGO
The one hiding behind their owner's legs

LIBRA
The one who always wears the cutest—and trendiest—sweaters

SCORPIO
The one who gets a little too "friendly" with every other dog

SAGITTARIUS
The one whose nose is glued to every other dog's butt

CAPRICORN
The one who territorially pees on people's shoes

AQUARIUS
The one staring off into space and barking at nothing

PISCES
The one pooping in a corner

✴

CHAPTER 6

The Signs and Their Homes

As the saying goes, home is where the heart is. So the question here is: "How does each sign infuse their home with their heart?" For Taurus folks, it includes stocking up their space with cozy blankets, earthy-scented candles, and houseplants. For Pisces, it's more about filling rooms with art. Sagittarius might consider "home" to be a tent or camper that they can easily take from one cool travel destination to another. Different strokes for different folks, and different designs for different signs!

This chapter will answer all of your home-related zodiac questions: What sort of decor speaks to each sign? What kind of candle should you scour your favorite home goods section for if you're, say, a Libra? Basically, this chapter will give you all the info you need to make your spot as homey and celestially aligned as possible—it's like astrological feng shui! So whether you're in a NYC studio or a McMansion in the countryside, there's something in here that will help you make your house, apartment, condo, RV, or whatever else you live in into a home. And anyway, don't you want to know what abstract wall art your sign is?!

The signs and their childhood bedrooms

ARIES

Clothes strewn everywhere, and aggressively bright-colored walls

TAURUS

Lots of fluffy pillows and— of course— string lights

GEMINI

Tiger Beat posters. *Everywhere.*

CANCER

Lots of pictures of friends and family

LEO

Posters of pop stars cover every inch of the wall

VIRGO

Absolutely pristine, even despite teen angst

LIBRA

Definitely has one of those canopy bed things

SCORPIO

There is a very prominent theme... perhaps Paris?

SAGITTARIUS

Has a trundle bed for *Epic. Sleepovers.*

CAPRICORN

Everything is in their favorite color. Like, literally everything.

AQUARIUS

No doubt has one of those race car beds

PISCES

Has bunk beds just for fun

ARIES

CHIC-YET-MODERN CHANDELIER
Full of light, and makes
a big statement

TAURUS

A VELVET CHAISE LOUNGE
Makes anywhere cozier

LEO

PERUVIAN WALL MIRROR
A beautiful frame for a
gorgeous reflection!

VIRGO

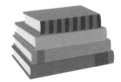

COFFEE TABLE BOOKS
Oh so cultured, and very
aesthetically pleasing

SAGITTARIUS

STRING LIGHTS
Fun, cheerful, and just a
pinch of mystical

CAPRICORN

VINTAGE OAK COFFEE TABLE
Sturdy, dependable, and
absolutely classic

home decor

GEMINI

MULTIFUNCTIONAL FLOOR POUF
Changeable, fun, and
has ~many sides~

CANCER

FINE CHINA DINNERWARE SET
Delicate, but keeps
everybody happy and fed

LIBRA

A CANDELABRA CACTUS
Beautifies and livens up any room!

SCORPIO

FLOOR LAMP
Moody, sleek, and mood-setting

AQUARIUS

MODERN VASE
Fabulously abstract and artistic

PISCES

SHAG RUG
Soft, comforting, and catches
other people's spills

ARIES

LOFT APARTMENT

TAURUS

COTTAGE

LEO

PENTHOUSE

VIRGO

BROWNSTONE

SAGITTARIUS

AIRSTREAM

CAPRICORN

COLONIAL

types of houses

GEMINI

CONTEMPORARY

CANCER

FARMHOUSE

LIBRA

VICTORIAN

SCORPIO

TUDOR

AQUARIUS

TINY HOME

PISCES

CAPE COD

The signs and their bookshelves

ARIES
Lots of different genres, and everything's half-read

TAURUS
50 percent romance novels, 50 percent their favorite celebs' cookbooks

GEMINI
All the latest trendy reads and bestsellers

CANCER
Mostly just half-finished self-help books

LEO
Lots and *lots* of celeb tell-alls

VIRGO
All the classics (and trust that they have read *all of them*)

LIBRA
Mostly just art books, TBH

SCORPIO
A borderline concerning number of books on cults...?

SAGITTARIUS
Books on philosophy, psychology, and the occasional romance novel

CAPRICORN
Lots of successful people's autobiographies and a manifestation journal

AQUARIUS
They've got poetry, books on aliens... they've got it all!

PISCES
Lots of books on spiritualism (and a couple romance novels)

The signs and their doormats

ARIES

"GO AWAY" and in small letters, "No, wait, come back!"

TAURUS

Handwoven, yet durable, and it's made of 100 percent recycled materials

GEMINI

It just says "Hi!" a bunch and that's the whole pattern

CANCER

The iconic "Welcome" in curly font

LEO

Something like "TAKE YOUR SHOES OFF!!!"

VIRGO

Neutral-colored and understated, perfectly complementing the decor of the house

LIBRA

Definitely has some sort of pattern printed on it

SCORPIO

"Enter at your own risk."

SAGITTARIUS

One that says "Hi" or "Bye" depending on what side you're facing

CAPRICORN

"WELCOME! Just kidding, please leave."

AQUARIUS

Braided and boho, rest assured

PISCES

Something personalized, like one that has their pet's photo on it

The signs and the countries

ARIES

JAPAN
Colorful, exhilarating,
and fast-paced

TAURUS

SWITZERLAND
Peaceful landscapes, kind
people, and *amazing* chocolate

LEO

SPAIN
Sunny, welcoming, and
has super fun nightlife

VIRGO

SINGAPORE
Small, efficient, and well-kept

SAGITTARIUS

AUSTRALIA
Has everything from the Great
Barrier Reef to the Outback

CAPRICORN

SCOTLAND
Lush, historical, and full of charm

they'd most like to live in

GEMINI

PERU
Full of food, culture, and wild terrain

CANCER

CANADA
People are kind and the outdoors is right there!

LIBRA

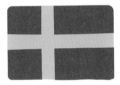

SWEDEN
Lots of design, scenery, and good work-life balance

SCORPIO

GERMANY
Plenty of villages and little markets to get lost in

AQUARIUS

NEW ZEALAND
Progressive, pastoral, and spacious

PISCES

FINLAND
Happy, charitable, and aesthetic

ARIES

A debatably creepy bobblehead

TAURUS

A hand-painted rock from their favorite beach

LEO

Cute lil' animal-shaped erasers

VIRGO

A tiny globe that actually spins

SAGITTARIUS

A little clay devil dipped in glitter

CAPRICORN

A ceramic piggy bank they painted when they were a kid

knickknacks

GEMINI

A teeny-tiny disco ball

CANCER

A seashell with glued-on googly eyes

LIBRA

A chunk of rose quartz

SCORPIO

A little castle made of Legos that you *really* don't wanna step on

AQUARIUS

A rubber band ball they've accumulated over the years

PISCES

A jar of handwritten affirmations

The signs and their morning routines

ARIES

Wakes up. Screams into pillow. Moves on with the day.

TAURUS

Three words: Elaborate. Skincare. Routine.

GEMINI

Scrolls through TikTok for thirty minutes before getting out of bed

CANCER

Cooks a delicious breakfast and, of course, *Instagram*s it

LEO

Recites positive affirmations to themselves in the mirror

VIRGO

Lights a candle and listens to their favorite podcast

LIBRA

Waters their plants, makes coffee, and generally romanticizes their morning

SCORPIO

Deeply stares into the void while they shower

SAGITTARIUS

Does some yoga (most notably the Sun Salutation)

CAPRICORN

Checks their email

AQUARIUS

Sleeps through the alarm

PISCES

Follows a guided meditation on *YouTube*

The signs as wall art

ARIES

Let's just say splatter paint is... *involved*

TAURUS

An oil painting of an Italian countryside

GEMINI

A nighttime city skyline reflected in water

CANCER

Something with a strong beach motif

LEO

Something undoubtedly gold and glittery

VIRGO

Something minimalist with a "color pop" of beige

LIBRA

Literally just a mirror

SCORPIO

A debatably haunted Victorian portrait that they thrifted

SAGITTARIUS

A motivational poster they got on *Amazon*

CAPRICORN

A framed dollar bill that holds some sentimental value

AQUARIUS

A movie poster they've had since they were a teen

PISCES

A tapestry that's fun to look at when they're...uh... bored

ARIES

TEDDY BEAR CACTUS

TAURUS

BEGONIA

LEO

MONSTERA

VIRGO

FIDDLE-LEAF FIG

SAGITTARIUS

PILEA

CAPRICORN

POTHOS

as houseplants

GEMINI

SNAKE PLANT

CANCER

MOTH ORCHID

LIBRA

PEACE LILY

SCORPIO

VENUS FLYTRAP

AQUARIUS

ZZ PLANT

PISCES

LUCKY BAMBOO

The signs and what you'll find

ARIES

Lots of Post-its of regularly ignored reminders

TAURUS

Lots of arts and crafts supplies!!!

LEO

Lots of pictures of them with their friends and family

VIRGO

A color-coordinated planner

SAGITTARIUS

The only thing on it is their laptop, which is absolutely smothered in stickers

CAPRICORN

Plenty of empty coffee mugs that somehow keep accumulating

on (or in) their home desks

GEMINI

A drawer full of candy (and candy wrappers)

CANCER

A plant or two to liven things up

LIBRA

A moody desk lamp for when inspiration strikes at 2 a.m.

SCORPIO

A lit candle to "center them"

AQUARIUS

A stack of mail that's been sitting there for a month

PISCES

Hand lotion at the ready to ~stay moisturized~

The signs

ARIES

CINNAMON THREE-WICK
Dynamic, strong-willed, so deliriously spicy that you can almost taste the aroma

TAURUS

PINE-SCENTED WOOD WICK
Earthy, nostalgic, instantly makes everyone feel comfy and cozy

LEO

RAINBOW DRIP
Zany, showstopping, looks good literally anywhere and with anything

VIRGO

LAVENDER
Pure, elegant, very woodland-fairy-meets-period-piece-love-interest

SAGITTARIUS

BUBBLE CUBE
Cute, charming, on trend (as always)

CAPRICORN

TAPER
Classic, revered, looks great in a dimly lit library or study

as candles

GEMINI

DOUBLE-ENDED TWISTY
Weird; colorful; that friend
who's really fun on nights out...
up until around midnight, and
then you have to babysit them

CANCER

GODDESS
Feminine, artistic, big
Goddess Energy all around

LIBRA

ROSE QUARTZ–INFUSED
Delicate, dainty, can—and
will—steal your lover

SCORPIO

PRAYER
Intentional, mystical, not
to be messed with

AQUARIUS

BIRTHDAY
Quirky, joyful, unafraid to
be a little different

PISCES

FLOATING TEALIGHT
Spiritual, calming, straight
out of a romance novel

✳

CHAPTER 7

The Signs and Their Jobs

Since you spend, ya know, a hefty chunk of your life enveloped in the workforce, it only makes sense to take a step back and think about your career choices from an astrological perspective. For example, cosmically speaking, it would make *zero sense* for a Sagittarius to go into some regular shmegular desk job where they crunch numbers all day. These archers need *variety*. On the other hand, for an organized and analytical Virgo, crunching numbers might honestly be therapeutic! And you won't find Capricorn in an unconventional trade or a cubicle: They'll be sitting in the huge corner office marked "Boss."

In this chapter, you'll discover each of the twelve signs' dream jobs, what their best interview outfits are, what niche jobs they'd actually be pretty good at, and—of course—how they'd reply to passive-aggressive work emails....And *waaaaay* more, obvi. So if you're at a bit of a career crossroads or have found yourself wondering about what side hustle might be a great fit for you, astrology can be more enlightening than you'd ever considered! Now, let's see what the stars say about a raise...

The signs in a meeting

ARIES
Is giving the presentation

TAURUS
Dozes in and out of sleep every five minutes or so

GEMINI
"Okay, so here's what I'm thinking..."

CANCER
"Don't worry, I'm taking notes."

LEO
Shows up late, iced coffee in hand

VIRGO
Is the one helping when the PowerPoint freezes

LIBRA
"Has anyone seen the laser pointer?"

SCORPIO
Secretly stole the laser pointer

SAGITTARIUS
Video calls in since they're on the other side of the continent for some reason

CAPRICORN
"We need to get our numbers up for Q4..."

AQUARIUS
Furiously doodles on notepad

PISCES
Raises hand to speak
Doesn't get called on

The signs and

ARIES

CEO
Gets to be in charge!

TAURUS

CHEF
Gets to be surrounded by food!

LEO

MOVIE STAR
Gets to be rich and famous!

VIRGO

NOVELIST
Gets to write stories every day!

SAGITTARIUS

TRAVEL WRITER
Gets to see the world
professionally!

CAPRICORN

PRESIDENT
Gets to lead a nation!

their dream jobs

GEMINI

TALK SHOW HOST
Gets to talk to cool people!

CANCER

ZOOLOGIST
Gets to care for wild animals!

LIBRA

FASHION DESIGNER
Gets to create their dream clothes!

SCORPIO

ARTIST
Gets to create beautiful art!

AQUARIUS

ASTRONAUT
Gets to go to space!

PISCES

POET
Gets to write about
feelings every day!

The signs and the niche jobs

ARIES

DOG TRAINER
Gets to work with dogs!!!

TAURUS

SOMMELIER
Gets to taste the finest wines!

LEO

TOUR GUIDE
Gets to travel and talk!

VIRGO

LIBRARIAN
Gets to read in PEACE!!!

SAGITTARIUS

PARK RANGER
Gets to be outside every day!

CAPRICORN

WEDDING PLANNER
Gets to plan other people's lives!

they'd actually be pretty good at

GEMINI

PODCASTER
Gets to talk professionally!

CANCER

DOULA
Gets to help deliver babies!

LIBRA

FLORIST
Gets to be around beautiful blooms!

SCORPIO

MARINE BIOLOGIST
Gets to work with sea creatures!

AQUARIUS

REIKI HEALER
Gets to be spiritual professionally!

PISCES

ART THERAPIST
Gets to paint *and* help people!

The signs making small talk with their coworkers

ARIES

*"Soooo...*I went on a fabulous date this weekend..."

TAURUS

"The weather this whole week has been perfect...not too hot, not too cold!"

GEMINI

"OMG, did you hear about Debbie in Sales?!"

CANCER

"How are your kids? I saw they're off to summer camp this week!"

LEO

Shows you their *Instagram* post of "a wild night" they had recently

VIRGO

"Finishing up those reports you asked for!"

LIBRA

"So how's that big presentation of yours coming along?"

SCORPIO

Silence

SAGITTARIUS

"I had the *wildest* weekend. Like, you're actually not even gonna believe it..."

CAPRICORN

Refills the water cooler because no one else will

AQUARIUS

"Have you heard of this artist? I'm going to their gallery opening tonight..."

PISCES

"How are you today? Making time for some self-care, I hope!"

The signs replying to an email

ARIES

Responds "Just following up..." literally two hours after sending original email

TAURUS

"Sorry for the late reply..."

GEMINI

Whatever it is, rest assured that there are *lots* of exclamation points!!!!!!!

CANCER

Accidentally replies all and subsequently has a nervous breakdown

LEO

"Thank you for circling back! Your message got lost in my overflowing inbox..."

VIRGO

Responds within five minutes, guaranteed

LIBRA

"Hope this email finds you well!"

SCORPIO

"Going forward, let's try to do this differently..."

SAGITTARIUS

Automatic out-of-office reply

CAPRICORN

"As per my last email..."

AQUARIUS

Says "See attached" but forgets to attach files

PISCES

"Hope you had a restful weekend!"

The signs and gifts they

ARIES

A mug that says something generic like "Stay away until I've had my coffee"

TAURUS

A lavender-scented bath bomb

LEO

Patterned socks with lil' wreaths on them

VIRGO

A bar of handmade artisanal soap

SAGITTARIUS

Their favorite hot sauce

CAPRICORN

A $20 bill

give at a work holiday party

GEMINI

A calendar of cats dressed like humans

CANCER

A box of their famous homemade cookies

LIBRA

A simple-yet-effective Starbucks gift card

SCORPIO

A popcorn maker

AQUARIUS

A big ol' bag of coffee they bought last minute at the nearby CVS

PISCES

A teeny-tiny baby succulent

The signs and their

ARIES

BURRITO BOWL

TAURUS

BAGEL WITH CREAM CHEESE

LEO

KALE SALAD

VIRGO

POKE BOWL

SAGITTARIUS

FALAFEL AND HUMMUS

CAPRICORN

LAST NIGHT'S LEFTOVERS

go-to work lunches

GEMINI

CAESAR SALAD

CANCER

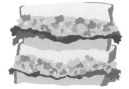

A RATHER PUNGENT TUNA SALAD
SANDWICH

LIBRA

PEANUT BUTTER AND JELLY SANDWICH

SCORPIO

SOUP FROM THE LOCAL SALAD BAR

AQUARIUS

QUESTIONABLE SUSHI FROM THE
GROCERY STORE

PISCES

BOWL OF CHILI

The signs as interns

ARIES
Makes everything—like, *everything*—a competition with the other interns

TAURUS
Triple-checks everyone's coffee order

GEMINI
Spills everyone's coffee order

CANCER
Helps themselves to a couple good stress cries in the bathroom

LEO
Constantly confuses the term "networking" with "flirting"

VIRGO
Secretly *loves* entering data into spreadsheets

LIBRA
Is always dressed to the absolute *nines*

SCORPIO
Has anxiety for a week prior to giving a presentation

SAGITTARIUS
Accidentally spreads coworker gossip not knowing it was gossip...???

CAPRICORN
Follows their mentor literally *everywhere*

AQUARIUS
Is only there because they lied on their resume

PISCES
Makes an effort to learn the names of everyone in the workplace

The signs working from home

ARIES
Turns camera and mic off during the Zoom meeting

TAURUS
Puts a *YouTube* video of a fireplace on in the background for ~ambience~

GEMINI
Desperately tries to coordinate Zoom social hours (to no avail)

CANCER
"Works" while simultaneously cooking the most ambitious meal you've ever seen

LEO
Goes for a daily midday run

VIRGO
Keeps a carefully organized calendar hung up on their wall in lieu of art

LIBRA
*Endlessly toggles between work tabs and *Twitter**

SCORPIO
Develops horrid posture from constantly working on their couch

SAGITTARIUS
Takes Zoom meetings exclusively from their car

CAPRICORN
Trades "business casual" for a "sweat suit"

AQUARIUS
Runs errands and just checks work emails periodically

PISCES
Always makes time for a lil' midday nap!

The signs and their

ARIES

PEPPERMINT MOCHA

TAURUS

MOCHA

LEO

ICED COFFEE

VIRGO

CHAI LATTE

SAGITTARIUS

FLAT WHITE

CAPRICORN

ONE SHOT OF ESPRESSO

at-work coffee orders

GEMINI

PUMPKIN SPICE LATTE

CANCER

MACCHIATO

LIBRA

MATCHA LATTE

SCORPIO

BLACK COFFEE

AQUARIUS

AMERICANO

PISCES

OAT MILK LATTE

The signs and their

ARIES

Something eye-catching and *red*

TAURUS

Scholarly-looking houndstooth pants

LEO

Funky pants + blazer = THE look!!!

VIRGO

Head-to-toe neutral tones

SAGITTARIUS

Gingham pants and a matching blazer

CAPRICORN

The classic slacks-and-blazer combo

interview outfit essentials

GEMINI

Understated, but wait for it...
there's a Statement Shoe™

CANCER

A distinguished argyle sweater
of sorts

LIBRA

A camel sweater over a white
button-down

SCORPIO

A black turtleneck à la
Steve Jobs

AQUARIUS

An electric blue sport coat

PISCES

Blue-light glasses to make them
look more "serious"

The signs as the boss

ARIES

Has been known to lose their temper in a boardroom or two

TAURUS

Scolds the intern for their own mistake

GEMINI

Gives the best motivational speeches

CANCER

Routinely checks in on the "emotional temperature" of their employees

LEO

Definitely owns a "World's Best Boss" mug that they bought themselves

VIRGO

Micromanages

LIBRA

Gives the most aesthetically pleasing presentations anyone has *ever* seen

SCORPIO

Silently elicits fear in the hearts of all their employees

SAGITTARIUS

Plans bimonthly team-building trips

CAPRICORN

Is somehow always in a meeting, and they like it that way

AQUARIUS

Constantly gives orders, but never remembers which orders they gave

PISCES

Cries every time they have to fire someone

✦

The Signs and Food

They say the way to someone's heart is through their belly, but what exactly should you put in each sign's belly to get to their heart?! For fire signs, maybe it's something with a lil' spicy kick to it. For water signs, they might prefer to drink it, swigging back some refreshing bevvies. Whatever it may be, it's time to dig into the different signs through the lens of delectable, delicious, and deliriously divine foods and drinks!

In this chapter, you'll learn about the signs as desserts, drinks, midnight snacks—you name it! You'll also discover what kind of restaurant fits each sign's vibe. For example, for a Virgo, a quaint, sun-lit café is perfect. For a Scorpio, a dimly lit joint with great appetizers and live jazz is the place to be. And you already *know* Taurus is all about anywhere that has good comfort food and a cozy fireplace! This chapter will definitely whet your appetite for both stars and *star*-ters alike. So grab some snacks and something to sip on, and sink your teeth into these tasty charts.

The signs and their favorite places to eat

ARIES
Any tapas restaurant where they can try bites of everything

TAURUS
Anywhere with comfort food, exposed brick, and/or a fireplace

GEMINI
Anywhere that's loud, trendy, and has "a scene"

CANCER
Anywhere with family-style food and good company

LEO
Anywhere that has good food and good photo ops

VIRGO
Any sort of quaint, sun-lit café

LIBRA
Anywhere (as long as it has three Michelin stars)

SCORPIO
Anywhere that's dimly lit, has live jazz, and offers a great post-dessert cappuccino

SAGITTARIUS
Any sort of food truck!!!

CAPRICORN
Anywhere that offers fancy three- (or more) course meals

AQUARIUS
Any sort of unexpected hole-in-the-wall spot

PISCES
Anywhere with an oceanfront view (preferably at sunset)

ARIES

ORANGE JUICE
Pure, fresh-squeezed
morning invigoration!!!

TAURUS

MILKSHAKE
Just pure sugary sweetness
that's beloved by all

LEO

COCA-COLA
Just plain classic, honestly

VIRGO

EARL GREY TEA
Somehow both soothing and
energizing at the same time???

SAGITTARIUS

APPLE CIDER
Sweet, nostalgic, and
strictly seasonal

CAPRICORN

BLACK COFFEE
A little bitter, but can
really get ya goin'!

as drinks

GEMINI

ICED COFFEE
An energizing on-the-go favorite

CANCER

HOT CHOCOLATE
Warm, comforting, and
feels like home

LIBRA

MATCHA LATTE
Trendy, caffeinated, and
just plain good for ya!

SCORPIO

CAPPUCCINO
Classy and *veeeeeery*
European-esque

AQUARIUS

SPRITE
Specifically the extra-spicy Sprite
they have at McDonald's

PISCES

CHAMOMILE TEA
Easily lulls you into dreamland

The signs as pizza

ARIES Pizza with crust that's a little burnt	**TAURUS** Chicago deep dish	**GEMINI** Pepperoni pizza
CANCER A good ol' New York slice	**LEO** Classic cheese pizza	**VIRGO** Greek pizza with extra olives
LIBRA California pizza	**SCORPIO** Neapolitan pizza	**SAGITTARIUS** Meat lover's pizza
CAPRICORN Sicilian pizza	**AQUARIUS** Lunchables pizza	**PISCES** Thin crust pizza

The signs and their favorite meals

ARIES
Tapas (so *lots* of delicious options)

TAURUS
Anything, as long as it has three courses minimum and a Michelin star

GEMINI
An ice cream sundae, hold the main course!!!

CANCER
Ramen

LEO
A big ol' cheeseburger and fries

VIRGO
A full Thanksgiving spread

LIBRA
A good ol' slice of pizza

SCORPIO
Spaghetti and meatballs

SAGITTARIUS
Literally just a Quesarito from Taco Bell

CAPRICORN
A nice, hearty, autumnal soup

AQUARIUS
Tacos, specifically ones from a food truck

PISCES
Chinese takeout

The signs as

ARIES

A cold slice of pizza

TAURUS

A piece of leftover birthday cake

LEO

Three-day-old Chinese food leftovers

VIRGO

Chocolate chip cookies straight from the cookie jar

SAGITTARIUS

A whole pint of Ben & Jerry's ice cream

CAPRICORN

A big bowl of buttery popcorn

midnight snacks

GEMINI

Macaroni and cheese (complete with powdered cheese packet)

CANCER

Chocolate-covered pretzels

LIBRA

A bag of sour cream and onion potato chips

SCORPIO

BBQ sauce–covered chicken wings (with a side of ranch)

AQUARIUS

Microwaved nachos

PISCES

Pizza rolls

ARIES

REESE'S PEANUT BUTTER CUPS

TAURUS

BUTTERFINGER

LEO

HOT TAMALES

VIRGO

M&M'S

SAGITTARIUS

SKITTLES

CAPRICORN

SNICKERS

their favorite candy

GEMINI

SOUR PATCH KIDS

CANCER

HERSHEY'S KISSES

LIBRA

STARBURSTS

SCORPIO

KIT KATS

AQUARIUS

SWEDISH FISH

PISCES

MILKY WAY

The signs as fortune cookie fortunes

ARIES
"Learn to slow down and sit in the sun."

TAURUS
"You yourself are a creature of abundance."

GEMINI
"There is no love more sacred than that between dear friends."

CANCER
"Your selfless nature will surely be rewarded."

LEO
"You cannot be tethered by others' self-imposed limits."

VIRGO
"Minding the details allows you to see bigger pictures."

LIBRA
"Stand firm on your holiest grounds."

SCORPIO
"Building walls around yourself will only keep out the love you so desire."

SAGITTARIUS
"Your spirit is called by the freest of winds."

CAPRICORN
"The richest people are not necessarily the wealthiest."

AQUARIUS
"Your mind is a door to possibilities that most fail to comprehend."

PISCES
"Strive not to carry love like an open wound."

The signs and the foods they wouldn't touch with a ten-foot pole

ARIES

Cilantro (and they'll make a whole scene about it)

TAURUS

Especially pungent Brussels sprouts

GEMINI

Candy corn

CANCER

Really wet olives

LEO

Mayonnaise

VIRGO

Mushrooms (for both texture and concept)

LIBRA

Tuna, for obvious reasons

SCORPIO

Lima beans

SAGITTARIUS

Eggplant...they *will* use the emoji though!

CAPRICORN

Cantaloupe, because it's "the worst of the melons"

AQUARIUS

Beets

PISCES

Black licorice

The signs

ARIES

CHOCOLATE CHIP COOKIE DOUGH

TAURUS

ROCKY ROAD

LEO

COOKIES 'N CREAM

VIRGO

MINT CHOCOLATE CHIP

SAGITTARIUS

MOOSE TRACKS

CAPRICORN

BUTTER PECAN

as ice cream

GEMINI

STRAWBERRY

CANCER

CAKE BATTER

LIBRA

NEAPOLITAN

SCORPIO

CHOCOLATE FUDGE BROWNIE

AQUARIUS

RAINBOW SHERBET

PISCES

COFFEE

ARIES

PIGS IN A BLANKET

TAURUS

SPINACH ARTICHOKE DIP

LEO

BUFFALO CHICKEN WINGS

VIRGO

CHIPS AND GUACAMOLE

SAGITTARIUS

MAC 'N CHEESE BITES

CAPRICORN

DEVILED EGGS

as appetizers

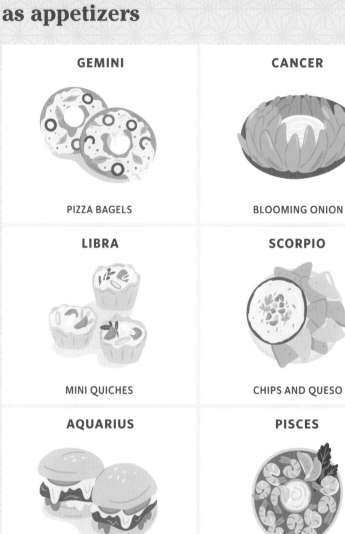

GEMINI

PIZZA BAGELS

CANCER

BLOOMING ONION

LIBRA

MINI QUICHES

SCORPIO

CHIPS AND QUESO

AQUARIUS

CHEESEBURGER SLIDERS

PISCES

SHRIMP COCKTAIL

The signs

ARIES

CHOCOLATE LAVA CAKE

TAURUS

PUMPKIN PIE

LEO

SUGAR COOKIES

VIRGO

TEXAS SHEET CAKE

SAGITTARIUS

PEANUT BUTTER COOKIES

CAPRICORN

TIRAMISU

as desserts

GEMINI

SEVEN-LAYER CHOCOLATE CAKE

CANCER

KEY LIME PIE

LIBRA

APPLE PIE

SCORPIO

ICE CREAM SUNDAE

AQUARIUS

WHOOPIE PIE

PISCES

CHEESECAKE

The signs and their comfort foods

ARIES
99¢ pizza

TAURUS
Grilled cheese and tomato soup

GEMINI
Mac 'n cheese

CANCER
Chicken noodle soup

LEO
Chicken and waffles

VIRGO
One (1) hot dog from a street cart

LIBRA
Spaghetti and meatballs

SCORPIO
Corn dogs

SAGITTARIUS
A cheeseburger and fries (perhaps with a milkshake)

CAPRICORN
A lightly toasted bagel

AQUARIUS
Loaded—like, *loaded*—nachos

PISCES
Chicken pot pie

CHAPTER 9

The Signs and Random Things (Because...Why Not?)

What haven't we covered? Oh, right—everything in between! Ever wondered what regrettable tattoo you are, according to your sign? Or which famous person serves as your sign's celebrity spokesperson? How about the signs as rom-coms, mythical creatures, or even yearbook superlatives?

The charts in this chapter are the ones that didn't necessarily fit anywhere else, but nonetheless feel important to include. They're also just plain fun! Like, who knew Libra is most likely the Best Dressed in school? Or that Capricorn is so Miranda Priestly from *The Devil Wears Prada*? Here's a recommendation for ya: Get a bunch of your friends together and compare your signs and the following random things. Have a great time reading about what kind of weird garage sale "treasure" your signs would be, and who would have the most fitting memoir title, according to the zodiac. Or laugh out loud while keeping these endearingly weird charts all to yourself. Regardless, things are gonna get a little freaky-deaky—in the best way. So without further ado, let's see what this chapter has in store for you (because...why not?!).

The signs as weird items found at garage sales

ARIES
An urn labeled "Ashes of my enemies"

TAURUS
An old couch with a very obvious stain

GEMINI
A large box filled to the brim with old Polly Pocket dolls

CANCER
Old Polaroids of someone else's precious moments

LEO
A painting of a cat playing chess against a rat

VIRGO
A "gently used" casket

LIBRA
A child's half-used diary

SCORPIO
An old, raggedy book titled *A Beginner's Guide to Taxidermy*

SAGITTARIUS
A chair made entirely out of tennis balls

CAPRICORN
A detailed oil painting of a centaur on a chaise lounge

AQUARIUS
A garden statue of a gnome riding a unicorn

PISCES
A prosthetic leg

The signs as

ARIES

PHOENIX

TAURUS

YETI

LEO

PEGASUS

VIRGO

UNICORN

SAGITTARIUS

DRAGON

CAPRICORN

GRIFFIN

mythical creatures

GEMINI

GNOME

CANCER

MERMAID

LIBRA

FAIRY

SCORPIO

KRAKEN

AQUARIUS

LOCH NESS MONSTER

PISCES

LEPRECHAUN

The signs as yearbook superlatives

ARIES
Most Likely to Move to Another Country Just Because

TAURUS
Most Likely to Marry Rich and Remain Generally Unbothered

GEMINI
Most Likely to Know the Gossip Before Anyone Else

CANCER
Best Person to Bring Home to Mom

LEO
Most Likely to Get Famous for Something Bizarre

VIRGO
Quietest, but When They Speak, Great Points Are Always Made

LIBRA
Best Dressed

SCORPIO
Most Likely to Somehow Survive an Apocalypse

SAGITTARIUS
Biggest Flirt

CAPRICORN
Most Likely to Make Six Figures Right Out of College

AQUARIUS
Most Enigmatic

PISCES
Most Likely to Make the World a Better Place

The signs as rom-coms

ARIES

10 Things I Hate About You

TAURUS

When Harry Met Sally...

GEMINI

Clueless

CANCER

Sleepless in Seattle

LEO

Notting Hill

VIRGO

You've Got Mail

LIBRA

Say Anything...

SCORPIO

Moonstruck

SAGITTARIUS

Dirty Dancing

CAPRICORN

Groundhog Day

AQUARIUS

Annie Hall

PISCES

The Notebook

The signs as

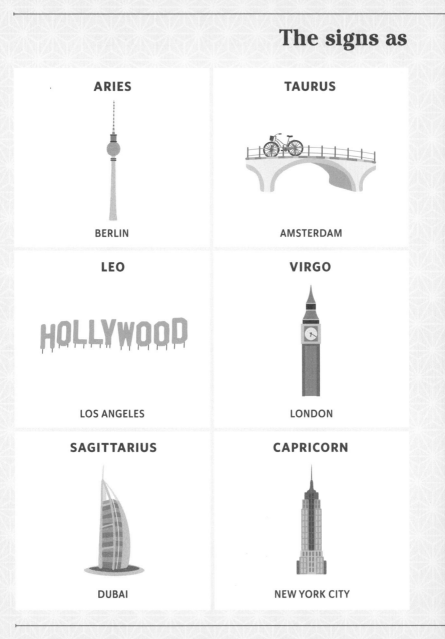

ARIES

BERLIN

TAURUS

AMSTERDAM

LEO

LOS ANGELES

VIRGO

LONDON

SAGITTARIUS

DUBAI

CAPRICORN

NEW YORK CITY